ASSASSINATE THE DEVIL

DR. SHONDA KIRK

Order this book online at www.trafford.com
or email orders@trafford.com

Most Trafford titles are also available at major online book retailers.

© Copyright 2021 Dr. Shonda Kirk.

All rights reserved. No part of this publication may be reproduced, stored in a retrieval system, or transmitted, in any form or by any means, electronic, mechanical, photocopying, recording, or otherwise, without the written prior permission of the author.

Print information available on the last page.

ISBN: 978-1-6987-0444-9 (sc)
ISBN: 978-1-6987-0446-3 (hc)
ISBN: 978-1-6987-0445-6 (e)

Library of Congress Control Number: 2020923127

Because of the dynamic nature of the Internet, any web addresses or links contained in this book may have changed since publication and may no longer be valid. The views expressed in this work are solely those of the author and do not necessarily reflect the views of the publisher, and the publisher hereby disclaims any responsibility for them.

Any people depicted in stock imagery provided by Getty Images are models, and such images are being used for illustrative purposes only.
Certain stock imagery © Getty Images.

KJV
Scripture taken from The Holy Bible, King James Version. Public Domain

Trafford rev. 12/29/2020

 www.trafford.com

North America & international
toll-free: 844-688-6899 (USA & Canada)
fax: 812 355 4082

Contents

Acknowledgments vii
Introduction xi

Prayer is A Weapon 1
Fasting Breaks Demonic Chains 11
The Word of God is A Trap for Satan 17
Worship Confuses The Enemy 23
Sowing a Seed Causes Satanic Confusion 29

My Prayer for You 35

Acknowledgments

I want to acknowledge COVID-19. If it wasn't for it coming to the earth, I do not think my faith would be as strong as it is. Before COVID-19 came, I was doing good in my faith. But one day, as I was in Vegas, God spoke to me on January 27, 2020, and said I need to faith-it-up the next months ahead. I begin to ponder, *Lord, I thought I was doing good*, but God said to me that I must be stronger in my faith. I look at my friends in the car, and I say I need to faith-it-up. I think I need to get a T-shirt to remind me through 2020. So when COVID-19 came, I realized that this is what God was speaking of. In my acknowledgments, I thank the COVID-19 being used to stretch me in greater faith.

Also, I would like to thank God for allowing me to write this book to help people know their adversary and begin to thank authority. God, I so love You, and I am glad You chose me to write this book.

Last but not least, I want to thank my husband and children. They have witnessed the Lord bring us through some things only He could. I am grateful to have them in my corner during these times of trusting in God and seeing Him work miracles. When the enemy tried to destroy our health, wealth, and life, the Lord came and lifted a standard against Him.

Introduction

I believe this book is to be written because many of the body of Christ members do not know their authority. Many people think that when they become a believer, they have the same life they had before. This is not true. When they become a believer, it is a fact that the life they have as a believer is so super ordinary of the supernatural power of God. Every believer must understand that is not the will of God for you to be in prison with things of the world or Satan have his way with you anymore. God's divine power has been given to His people to do the work of the ministry, and the ministry starts with us knowing who to release it in our lives first. This book will teach the body of Christ how to walk in their authority and what they must do to successfully win in every battle they may face.

Assassinate the devil!

PRAYER IS A WEAPON

I have found, being saved since 1995, a lot of people are very passive in the body of Christ, and they allow the enemy to come against Him in so many ways. I found that I must address in this book how I have faced many things and how the enemy thought that he could just run over me and do whatever he wanted, but I had to take a stand, especially as a child of the Most High God. I learned over the years that there's a special grace that God gives to His people that is authoritative from the heavens. There is a special anointing that I can believe in my heart that God has given me that will cause even Satan to shut his mouth when I want him to, and I have found through different points that I will share in this book that will help the body of Christ. There are things that we must come up with, and there are things that we must come out of. There are things that we must take dominion of, or we will live a life under the table, under the bus, and the enemy will wrack our brains to pieces.

I have found in the body of Christ that some of us do not know how important it is to know who we are, where we came from, and who lives within us. I want to take you to a story of how I grew up. I grew up in a hole in his church. I grew up learning how to make the outward part of me beautiful. I grew up where I had to wear a particular kind of clothes and in a particular way, but I had no power; meaning, I did not know how to get Satan off my head, mind, life, finances, everything that I possess. It was until I got in the word and began to make the word a revelation to me personally. I had to wake up through divorce, church hurt, being rejected. it through Brit being on the throne you can say in a bag in so many words

But I learned, through the word of God, how to walk with Him. I'm sorry so I introduced to some of you

And I give to most of you the word spoken in Matthew 12. It says this: The kingdom of God suffered violence, but the violent shall take it by force. It was until I made the word a violent choice from heaven that I will walk in kingdom authority. It was when I took the word and began to say "I am walking in the kingdom of God," and I have to understand that there will be some things that I may suffer through, but I am to open up my mouth and be violent and take authority over everything in my life that is not lining up to the word of God. There are some of you who are reading this right now and your life is jacked up, torn, and your mind is so confused, but I come to let you know today that God is not the author of confusion. In fact, I must let you know he's not confusing you. He's not harassing you. He's not taking anything from you. He is the God of everything you need. As we look at Genesis 1:26, we can see that God created us in His image and after His likeness. He created us to take authority because we have God in us, and everything Godhead is always first in our lives, and so therefore, because we are God's image and God's headship is within us, we can now possess the things that we are supposed to possess spiritually and naturally. We were never supposed to be the tail. We were never supposed to be at the end of a thing. We were supposed to always take refuge and take dominion from the beginning, but because of our sin nature, we had to repent and get it together and receive the grace of God. We can only understand now that we have to forget the things behind us and press toward the things before us. God has brought us into a place of taking and assassinating the enemy like never before. You must learn to assassinate. With the word you must learn to OSAS and ate the enemy with the word the word assassinate the enemy

How do we assassinate the enemy? We first begin to pray. The devil hates it when you pray. the devil hate when you open your mouth because when you open your mouth the enemy has to run if you read Matthew for everything the devil told Jesus he began to give Jesus he begin to give the devil the word he began to give the devil the word if you are is hungry Jesus turn the stones into bread

And Jesus began to say man shall not live on bread alone but by everything that comes out of the mouth of God. Everything Jesus spoke was the word. Everything he lived for is the word. So what should I do when the enemy seems to be on my head, on my children, on my marriage, on my finances, on my job? You must first understand that prayer is your weapon against the enemy.

If there is anything that I know to do, it is to pray in faith, and God answers me. It is the prayers, the Bible says. and James that avail if much

When we pray, we literally call the heavens to open up and do a miracle on earth for us, to call the enemy to crumble. Prayer is the communication of God. It is having communion with the Father. It is taking your all and laying them at the altar and entering into the Holy of Holies so you can be in the very presence of the Father. There is a place in God, in prayer, that the enemy cannot do well.

there is a place in prayer that God calls your man to feel as if it's not there is a place in prayer that would calls a Psalms 91 that

You dwell in the secret place of the Almighty God, and He protects you from all evil, and when you leave that place, you begin to walk supernaturally upon the earth. that will be a weapon up on the

Every believer must decide to walk in the divine lifestyle of prayers and faith. I'm not talking about just prayers. Prayers are good. I can pray a general religious prayer, but I'm talking about a prayer that is in faith. that will calls a ignition igniting of your spirit to come awaken to call you to walk in a place that you never walk before that you know God has created you to walk in every single day you awake off of your prep call a prank call a Pratt time a proud moment what calls Satan to run from you

Every time you pray, you are releasing a weapon that dispels the work of the enemy. he's a tax and his obstacles

The Bible says in Ephesians 6 that prayer is an armor. You cannot dismiss prayers. as I believe up because Prayer is the very unknotting prayer is the very unknotting where God dwells where his angels dwell

And when you pray, angels are being released. but for your day the best way to calls the weapon of prayer to work is in your life is commanding the mall the morning to come commanding your morning commanding. When you command your morning you are releasing an expectation in the atmosphere so God Kim release a greater anointing for the day and then when you go out your day things begin to happen supernaturally souls begin to get save everything that you do in prayer it actually comes out in your date went out but you begin to pray and not sees God is obligated to your prayer up because he said if you come to me all year who I have a laden I'm going to get your rest you will get rested prayer you will get pizza in prayer you were gay establishing your very being in prep because were pretty is that where an anointing isWhere in a 19 years that it's where an assignment is so win an assignment is released on your life you are understand why you were create it

And when you understand why you were created, you would then know that prayer is a weapon against Satan. It will assassinate that devil. The devil would be mad when you pray. When you pray, that devil has to run because you're communicating with God and not with him. Therefore, when you release the word, he cannot come against it because the word is powerful. Hebrew said is sharper than any two edge sword cutting through the very soul and body the mind the wheel of a person and so does Soul and that's win the weapon a prayer would be a force against the pits of hell

And the pits of hell cannot come against prayer. The enemy may try, but he cannot win. God loves it when we pray because we are communicating with him. not there a different prayer statue can pray a prayer of thanksgiving a prayer and supplication of a prayer hallelujah of rejoicing there's many different prayers but the prayers of the heart the prayer of day that caused him to be a man that that was the lover of God he was the lover of God a prayer what calls your mind to change.

Another way that prayer is a weapon is when you give your cares to the Lord and you allow Him to assassinate the devil for you. When you pray, you must release yourself from trying to fix the problem and allow your faith in God to fix the problem. When you pray, you are communing with God; you're talking with Him. When you come to him, He listens. When are you quiet and you listen to Him speak, He can give you insight of things that He wants to speak to you so you would know the devices, the tricks, the schemes, the things that the enemy will try to put upon you. You will see clearly, and you will not be tricked by the enemy. The enemy's job is to confuse, abuse, irritate, aggravate you, to cause you to be up and down like a roller coaster, so you can't focus on what God has planned for your life. In this season that you are praying to God, you are then a laminating and assassinating the devil. He cannot come to you and do whatever he wants to do because you are on assignment for God. When you pray, you call the fire of heaven, like Elijah did on the false prophets, to calm down and begin to do a work in your life and also to dispel and counter the works of Satan. He has no authority but what we give him. Prayer is a weapon to call the enemy to understand that the kingdom of God suffers violence, but the violent will take it by force. You know who you are, and you know that even the hands of God is upon your life to do exploits for the kingdom. The kingdom was never to be made as a place that was passive. Nothing in God's kingdom or God is passive. God has come to bring life to His people. His will is our will, and His will to for us to know His kingdom is all that we have to come against our enemy.

The enemy's job each day is to distract us, for us not to fulfill what God has called us for. It is not about what you know about God, but it is about doing what the Bible says, to walk with God each day. When we do not pray, we are asking to be in the ring of the enemy by ourselves. Prayer is a healer of the body. Prayer causes the enemy to step back and look at you and say, "You can touch this." Don't be confused, prayer is simply talking to God and Him talking to you. Prayer becomes a weapon when we learn how to use it. In Ephesians 6, it says that we are to hold on to prayer. Prayer is an armor that protects as the other armors of the Lord mentioned in Ephesians 6. The breastplate of righteousness, the helmet of salvation, the gospel of peace, the shield of faith, the belt of truth, etc.— all of these have a specific function, but they all are for our protection, a weapon against the enemy. To assassinate means to kill, murder, humiliate that punk so he will never think he has dominion over your life or your family. Most people are defeated because they do not know how to operate the armor God has given to them, and they live a life of defeat. In this time and season we are in, in the body of Christ, we must desire to be about the Father's business to change our life and those around us. It is not a time for us to desire to live passively but to live aggressively. There was nothing passive about Jesus. He always knew His Father who was in Him, and He was uncompromisable and caring to those He met. Jesus was the same everywhere. He meant and let the enemies know he was not to be walked over. He spent time in prayer with God, and once He did, He came from the mountain to the people and began to do the work of the ministry. He knew prayer was His weapon daily, and this made His life with His Father immensely powerful each day. Jesus was not your average carpenter boy, but He knew how to walk in the power of God and use prayer as a weapon in His life.

Prayer, as your weapon, teaches you there is power in Jesus's name!

FASTING BREAKS DEMONIC CHAINS

What is fasting? Basically, fasting is abstaining from food for a time. Fasting is used by some people to lose weight, committing to certain meal plans, and for some people, fasting is for leisure and not to be taken seriously.

When God speaks of fasting, He lets us know that His Son Jesus prayed and fasted for forty days, Matthew 4, and He trusted God. We must also trust God when we pray and fast because He is in control. Prayer helps build our relationship with God, and we commune with Him to get to know Him better. Prayer is the foundation of God. Without prayer, we cannot get to know God. God does nothing without prayer. I remember growing up in North Carolina and the mothers of the church would be so strict on making sure new believers have a prayer life. They would say to us, "Little prayer, little power. Much prayer, much power." I have held on to this forever, and this has been my life.

It's amazing how having a relationship with God will change your whole life. It is prayer that keeps you in the things of God. To learn to assassinate the devil, you must have a lifestyle of prayer. The enemy is not concerned with how much Bible you read and how often you go to church. The enemy is scared when you begin to speak out in the open of what the Bible says. When we assassinate the devil in prayer, we cry out to the Lord to tear down altars of the enemy. The altars of the devil are built to stop the work of the Lord. When God has given you His power, He wants you to use it, and that is not being quiet by any means but speaking the word of the Lord. A way to make the devil mad is by quoting the scriptures. The word gives life to all, and it comes from your mouth. From your mouth, it produces great deliverance. The devil cannot stop you. The Bible says the devil or Satan is the father of lies. The authority that God has given His people is for us to know that prayer and fasting causes changes in our life. It causes us to die of ourselves to be more like Jesus. To be like Jesus, we must have a heart for Christ and do the work He has called us to do. It is not about being scared of your enemy but about knowing that when you open your mouth, the enemy runs. We have the authority to tell the devil where to go and never to come back ever again. When you know who you are, you can move forward in your life and leave the enemy behind you. I remember Jesus told Satan to get behind him. We should tell the enemy he has no power and he must die by fire! The Lord Jesus lets us know we are His handiwork in Ephesians 2:10. This means God has made us the way we He wants us to be. God does not know defeat. God does not know of a place where the enemy is allowed to take over what He has created. We must be the same way. We can't allow the enemy to come in when he wants and do what he wants to us. The Bible says that Satan was a liar from the beginning, and he is a liar now. The enemy is not your friend, and your job is to make sure you dispel his lies and all he does to stop you progress.

Prayer is a weapon that is spoken from heaven and is let loose upon the earth. In Ephesians 6, God speaks of the armor of him and how prayer is one of our armors against the wiles of the devil.

When the devil is roaring like a lion, you must have a word in you mouth. The armor of the Lord is the armor that is meant to protect you from all evil. The armor must be upon us all the time to be able to cancel the works of Satan. I remember when one of my sons was young and he could talk. He used to say to my husband and me, "The devil is telling me not to obey you and Dad." When he would tell me that, I would tell him to say "Jesus" and "the blood." You, the reader, may not understand what I am saying. The Bible says there is power in the name of Jesus. So I take this word and begin to say "Jesus," and things begin to take place. The Bible says the name of Jesus is a strong tower where the righteous run to, to be safe. We must know that with prayer, we are in a safe place with God, a place where demons tremble by the name of Jesus. When we pray, we ignite what the heavens is waiting for us to release by the words that cause the earth to shake.

Many people pray but do not fast. Although some things come by praying and fasting, its releasing power only comes from the Lord. Praying and fasting gives you more supernatural strength to endure as a good soldier. It takes the hand of God to help His children pray and fast while they call on His name and trust Him. Proverbs 3:5 says to trust in the Lord with all your heart and do not lean on your own understanding but acknowledge Him in all your ways. The trust must be in the Lord when we pray and fast to destroy demonic attacks. We will have demonic attacks, but the truth is once we know that power of Almighty God, we operate in the ways He gives us to defeat the enemy.

Demonic spirits come to bring fear and intimidation. Demons do not come to bring peace but to make us fail and not succeed in our walk with Christ. There is nothing that can stop us from doing anything in our lives that God has called us to do. The only enemy is the enemy of ourselves that we are familiar with. Satan can only be used against us when we allow Him to operate in our old mindset. Demons are not what God wants us to fear, but He wants us to fear Him. God says in His word, in the book of Proverbs, that the beginning of wisdom is to fear the Lord. It is by God's grace and His power that we go forth and complete the assignment He has on our lives. The assignment is not of any grief, but it is of God's power. It is of the will of God, and it is the will of heaven. Praying and fasting against demonic attacks causes miracles, signs, and wonders.

THE WORD OF GOD IS A TRAP FOR SATAN

The word of God is what Jesus used in Matthew 4 to trap the enemy to the point where he was confused. Although the enemy will try to use the word of God on you, he can never use it properly because he hates God and His word. How do we trap the enemy with God's word? Is it us just reading the Bible every day? Is it us quoting scriptures and being so religious? No, it is not. It is when we read the word and apply the word. Reading the word is a wonderful thing to do, and yes, we are to read the Bible every day. We are to also study the word of God so we do not sin against God. The Bible is our road map to life, but it is nothing to take lightly. I remember when COVID-19 came in my home, and I could just smell evil and death. It was not a shock to me how the enemy tries to attack my family. It came to two of my family members, and I begin to say, "DIE BY FIRE!" But then I had to speak the word, and the Bible says in Matthew 8:17 that every sickness and every disease, God has taken, and I or my family do not have them anymore. As God's people, we are not partakers of sickness. We do not get sick. I can boldly say this because in this scripture, we can see God took it, so why do we have it? The Bible also says that "no weapon that is formed against me shall not prosper and every tongue that rises up against me shall be condemned." How do we come against the forces of sickness? We must first know the word of God, and God says we are healed. Sickness is a demon from hell. God has never intended us to be sick. We must curse sickness and proclaim we are healed. When weapons form, they cannot prosper according to Isaiah 54:17. So when we read the word, we must own the word and trap Satan with the word. We trap him when we speak the word aloud to come against the word he speaks in our minds. The mind is not saved, so when something that is not the word comes in, we must make sure we open our mouths and proclaim the gospel of Jesus Christ. The sixty-six books of the Bible have something in it we must partake of in situations we may face. This is why David said the word is "a lamp upon my feet and a light on my pathway" in Psalms 119. Without the word, you cannot be led with the light because the word leads you in a righteous pathway.

When COVID-19 came to my home, I could not stutter, I had to move quickly. I did not know the name of it when it was attacking my family in November 2019–February 2020, but I did know it was not of God. It was a file spirit and was looking to kill, steal, and destroy as John 10:10 says the enemy comes to do. But because I knew part b of John 10:10, this gave me hope. God came to bring life and that more abundantly. I could not think that what God had been teaching me all these years since I been saved could falter to the ground. It was in that life-or-death moment to my family. I chose life for my family. Immediately, I got the oil and began to command the enemy to get off them. I warred until I felt a release in the spirit. I covered them in oil and told the devil he had to release them and let them go. At that moment, I was trapping the enemy in God's spiritual trap. The words he spoke became of less value to me, the way my family looked did not matter, but I began to see them come out of the sickness before my eyes. They sweated, and the pain lessened. The satanic spirit came from the pits of hell. It brought pain, aches, hard breathing, cough, runny nose, fever, and most of all, torment. When I heard my family cries, I called on Jesus and began to speak what he spoke, that they would live and not die and declare the works of God. It was in that moment that I knew this was not a sickness unto death but a test of our faith and the word. Sooner or later, the demon had to release my family. and it the sweet by and by it was gone. I opened my front door as a prophetic move and commanded that sickness to leave and never come back. It has never come back again, and I praise God. What was the key to healing COVID-19? It was not fear of anything but faith that had everything. It was my faith in the word that caused the disease to leave my home. I held on to God's word despite the situation and what the enemy was saying. I did not look at the situation, but my eyes were fixed on God's word. When I did this, it trapped the enemy, and his words became null and void. There is no sickness that can stop the plan of God on our lives. It may come, but it cannot stay. Nothing can stop what God has ordained. It was in that moment I saw my family members arise like Lazarus. It was in that moment I saw my faith before my eyes and the sickness left. I believe every sickness and pain that is given to us is a demon. God knows we cannot work for him in any affliction. The most successful people will let you know, yes, things as sickness will come but must leave as nothing. It's not important what the enemy does. What is important is what we do when he comes. Jesus knew this, Matthew 4, when the enemy tried to twist His words. He gave the enemy the Bible to let him know He will only do as the word and His Father God has spoken. Jesus knew the word because He was the word. The word of God is the only thing that can trap Satan, and when we speak, the word "change" comes.

What does it mean to trap Satan? It means we take the word of God and we make the word our declaration to consume the lies of the enemy. The enemy is a defeated foe and has no power. God has all the power. When we speak the word, we trap him.

Our goal as believers of Christ is to make sure we understand we are not a friend of the devil. We hate what God hates and love what God loves. God do not love Satan, and we should not love him.

We trap the enemy when we speak the word. When we apply the word, it traps the hand of the enemy. Satan do not have any authority unless we give authority.

WORSHIP CONFUSES THE ENEMY

There have been many times I have been in certain situations and just begin to worship the Lord. When I would praise the Lord, my mind would not think on what the enemy was doing to come against my life. Worshipping God is given from your heart. Everyone cannot worship God because if they would, there could not be so many rebellious people coming against the place of Almighty God. Worship is a weapon that can be used to keep the enemy's mouth close. When we worship the King of kings and the Lord of lords, we put the enemy in place. As God's children, we have the authority to go against the demonic works of Satan.

Worship keeps us in a place of knowing that God has His hands upon us. In worship, we find ourselves in the places of the heavens. There is a place in worship that we can be in and move forward in places that we have never been in before. We go from glory to glory and faith to faith.

As a believer, we do not stay the same in God. Worship comes from the heart, and our hearts begin to give 100 percent to the Lord. When we are sold out, we give God all our hearts and minds.

Some people say they are sold out to God, but they are not willing to do what He asks them today. Everyone can praise God, but everyone cannot worship God. Worshippers are who Jesus is seeking for according to John 4. When Jesus spoke of this, He was looking for true worshippers who can worship Him in spirit and in truth. When we worship God, we die of ourselves, and we welcome Jesus to come in and pour out upon us. Worship is a weapon because the enemy do not want you to worship the God you serve. The enemy wants you to worship him and his ways with complaining but not with rearranging your life into another place. Worship is not anything you learn. It's something you do because you fall in love with God. We do it because, as His sons and daughters, we love Him dearly, and He loves us back. There are places in worship where God will shield you from the enemy. He will hide you where the enemy cannot locate you. God says he is a present help in the time of trouble. Psalms 91:1 tells us, as we stay in the secret place of the most high and abide, he, shadow of the enemy, will protect under the shadow of the Almighty, and nothing shall harm us. The weapon of worship and songs sang in hymns to the Lord are the songs of our heart. The songs become warfare before the Lord, and no evil can befall you come near your dwelling. When God hears our worship, the angels line up for battle, and they are waiting for the enemy to come. and they smitten his head. Whatever battle you are facing now, know this much: The Lord has lifted a standard against the enemy, and he is already defeated.

The Bible says in 2 Corinthians 10:4–5, the weapons of our warfare are mighty through God, through pulling down of every strong hold. We pull down imaginations that are not of God in the atmosphere; therefore, the enemy can't do what he wants to do. When we worship, we pull down demonic activities in high places trying to lay strongholds on your mind and lose things from your life. Worshipping God causes you to go to places in the spirit and surpass the natural above all. Worship burns the enemy's head and releases a place for God to dwell in your life forever and not just a moment. When you truly worship God as you should, you do not have any fear because God will protect His people because of worshipping Him. Worship is a weapon for you to force darkness away from you and your family. Worship him today!

SOWING A SEED CAUSES SATANIC CONFUSION

Many people do not look at seed sowing as a thing to do in the society we live in. Let's go back to Genesis 8:22, where the Bible says there is always a time for seed time and harvest. We must understand that when there is a seed that is being sown, the enemy is there to confuse you to not receive your harvest. Sowing causes you to release your faith and receive a greater outcome like never before.

When God gave Jesus to the world, this was the first seed, and no one else had never sown any other seed. Can you image giving your child for the kingdom or the world? Would you give your only child for the world? Abraham gave his son Isaac as a sacrifice to God, and God brought a ram in the bush for Abraham. Please understand when you release anything out of your hands, it means you trust God in all you do. Abraham trusted God, and God provided. When God gave Jesus, He knew that Jesus would be the perfect sacrifice for the world. The world needs to know that Jesus was the seed from God that made the enemy hate that God ever released Christ as the answer to the world. The Bible says in the book of John that Jesus was sent to destroy the works of the devil.

The seed of Jesus is destroying the works of the enemy because God sent His son on assignment.

What happens when we decide to sow a seed? Let's take money for example. When we give our tithe and offering, we break curses of poverty off our life. Malachi 3 says we are cursed with a curse. This means we put a curse on ourselves when we do not give to God. Where do curses come from? Curses come from the enemy, the devil. The devil is not cursing some of us. We are welcoming him when we curse ourselves. Sometimes people curse themselves, and they don't even know it. How do we curse ourselves? We curse ourselves by not allowing God's word to come to life in us and we choose not to obey. When it comes to finances, no one should be without anything financially if they are giving to the Lord. To burn satanic altars, we learn to walk in the word and live by the word, and the word works for us and not us sweating to make the word work. What we release out of our hands depends on what God releases out of His hands. The enemy becomes confused because he cannot figure out what you are smiling for in the midst of problems and you keep sowing a seed in the midst of all the hurts. When the enemy get confused, he does not know how to locate you, and this is where sowing comes into play. Confusion is known to be anything that is not settled or do not have a set place. Confusion, in other words, means to be unstable, double-minded, uncertain, puzzled, indecisive, hesitating, etc. These are all things that we do to the devil when we sow a seed because the root of the seed is when we sow in faith to God, and this causes the enemy to be perplexed. Our job as God's children is to make the enemy know we have our authority to shut down his tactics and tricks. When he tries to bring confusion, we send it back to him.

The main problem with most sons and daughters of God, they start off well, but when the attack comes, they do not operate in the spirit but the flesh, and this causes us to back in a cycle. We must be consistent in the process of sowing. We cannot afford to give our tithe and offering when it comes to worshiping God. Sowing is a form of worship, and when we give, we choose to worship God. Worship confuses the enemy, and when it's released, it causes miracles for the person sowing the seed.

My Prayer for You

Whoever you may be who is reading this book, my prayer for you is that you assassinate the devil. Each time you open up your mouth, he will be confused. God has not given you the spirit of fear but love, power, and a sound mind. You are a priority to God, and He has given you everything you need in this season to go forth and be a blessed man or woman of God. No devil in hell can stop you from doing the will of God in your life. The assassination starts now, and you shall befall every evil that tries to come near your dwelling. You are more than a conqueror, and no one, by any means, will be able to stop. I am a living witness that the devil is defeated and Jesus is Lord.

I love you.
Your Life Coach,
Dr. Shonda Kirk

CPSIA information can be obtained
at www.ICGtesting.com
Printed in the USA
LVHW110426030221
678219LV00007B/677